Schaum

Keynote Speller

Level One

By John W. Schaum
for Piano or Electronic Keyboard

Foreword

In order to reinforce the sight reading process, the Schaum Keynote Music Speller books enable the student to picture simultaneously the two elements of keyboard music reading, keyboard and notation, hence the name keynote.

By associating the tactile image of the keyboard with the image of the printed notation, the student learns to correlate the keyboard location with the note location. Withe the combined mental picture of key and note, the student will be better equipped to transfer the written knowledge of the Schaum Keynote Music Speller books to actual keyboard note reading. Faster music reading will be the result.

The staffs are always printed above the keyboard diagrams to simulate a real reading situation, since in practical performance the printed music is always above the keyboard. Thus, greater carry-over from note writing to actual sight-reading is promoted.

One of the greatest factors in learning is interest. The object of these writing books is to present the essentials of music reading in a manner that will intrigue and stimulate the student.

Schaum Publications, Inc.
10235 N. Port Washington Rd. • Mequon, WI 53092 • www.schaumpiano.net

© Copyright 1962, Renewed 1990 by Schaum Publications, Inc., Mequon, Wisconsin
International Copyright Secured • All Rights Reserved • Printed in U.S.A.
ISBN-13: 978-1-936098-03-3

CONTENTS LEVEL ONE
(A or Gr. 1)

All pages in this book are PERFORATED. If desired, pages may be removed and assigned individually.

CONTENTS PRIMER LEVEL

Lesson 1. Grand Staff

Pupil's Name..   Completion Date..

Assignment Date..   Grade or Star..

DIRECTIONS: The GRAND STAFF is a combination of the treble and bass staffs. Its range is shown below. Write letter names in the squares, place check marks on the keyboard diagram and draw connecting lines between keys and notes.

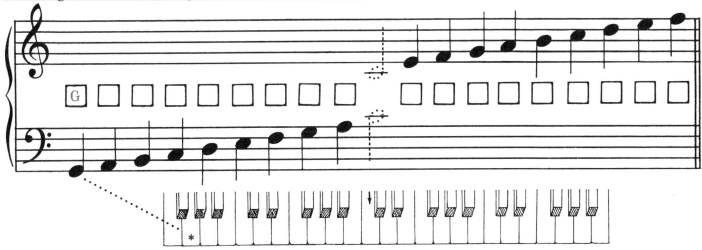

DIRECTIONS: The LINES of the GRAND STAFF are printed below. Write letter names in squares, place check marks on the keyboard diagram and draw connecting lines between keys and notes.

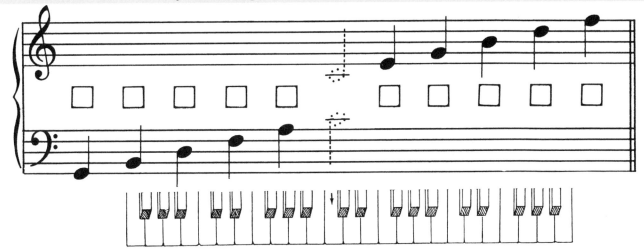

DIRECTIONS: The SPACES of the GRAND STAFF are printed below. Write letter names in squares, place check marks on keyboard diagram and draw connecting lines between keys and notes.

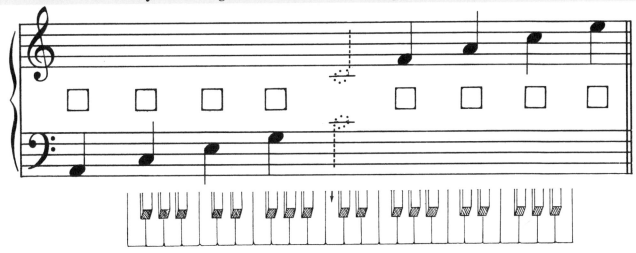

Teacher's Note: All Keynote Spelling Lessons are to be performed at the keyboard.

↓ Denotes Middle C

Lesson 2. Grand Staff Slogans

Pupil's Name.. *Completion Date*..

Assignment Date.. *Grade or Star*..

DIRECTIONS: Write letters in the squares, place check marks on the keyboard diagrams and draw connecting lines between keys and notes.

TREBLE LINES

Earth's Gravity Brings Descent Fast

TREBLE SPACES

F — A — C — E

BASS LINES

Giant Booster Drives Flying Astronaut

BASS SPACES

A Capsule Encircles Globe

↓ Denotes Middle C

Lesson 3. Correlating Slogans with Steps (Up)

Pupil's Name..

Assignment Date..

Completion Date..

Grade or Star...

The use of slogans in reading the lines and spaces of the treble and bass staffs is especially beneficial when correlated with step progression. The slogans can act as guide posts.

DIRECTIONS: Go UP two steps from each of the following notes by adding two whole notes. Consult the sample. Keep the slogans in mind. Join each step with a slur. Write letter names in the squares, place check marks on the keyboard diagrams and draw connecting lines between keys and notes.

Think: **E**arth's **G**ravity **B**rings **D**escent **F**ast

Think: **F** — **A** — **C** — **E**

Think: **G**iant **B**ooster **D**rives **F**lying **A**stronaut

Think: **A** **C**apsule **E**ncircles **G**lobe

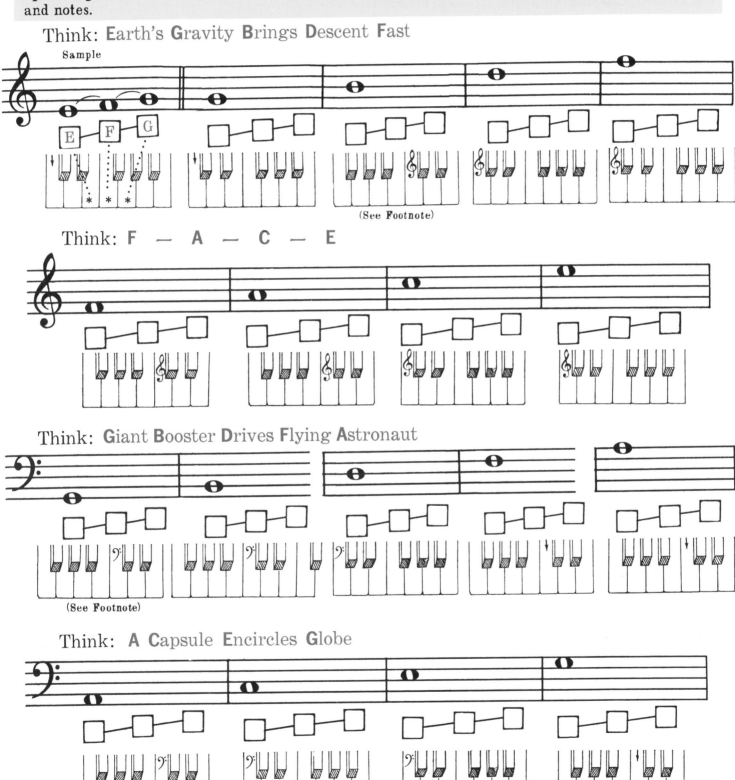

Note: The small treble clef 𝄞 over C on the keyboard diagram denotes Treble C (first C above middle C). The small bass clef 𝄢 over C indicates Bass C (first C below middle C).

⤓ Denotes Middle C

Lesson 4. Correlating Slogans with Steps (Down)

Pupil's Name.. Completion Date..

Assignment Date.. Grade or Star..

DIRECTIONS: Go DOWN two steps from each of the following notes by adding two whole notes. Study the sample. Keep the slogans in mind. Join each step with a slur. Write letter names in the squares, place check marks on the keyboard diagrams and draw connecting lines between keys and notes.

Think: **Earth's Gravity Brings Descent Fast**

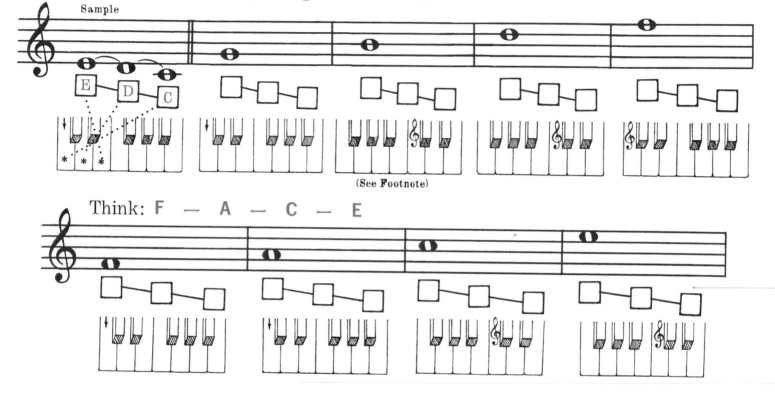

(See Footnote)

Think: **F — A — C — E**

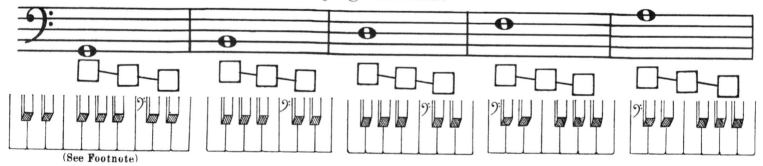

Think: **Giant Booster Drives Flying Astronaut**

(See Footnote)

Think: **A Capsule Encircles Globe**

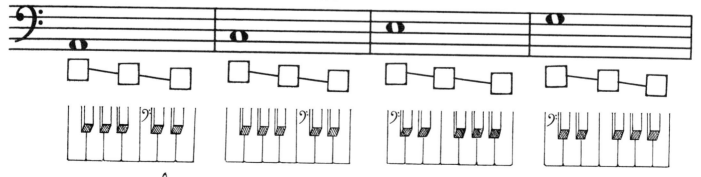

Note: The small treble clef 𝄞 over C on the keyboard diagram denotes Treble C (first C above middle C). The small bass clef 𝄢 over C indicates Bass C (first C below middle C).

↓ Denotes Middle C

Lesson 5. Grand Staff Spelling

Pupil's Name..   *Completion Date*..

Assignment Date..   *Grade or Star*..

DIRECTIONS: Write letter names in the squares, place check marks on the keyboard diagrams and draw connecting lines between keys and notes.

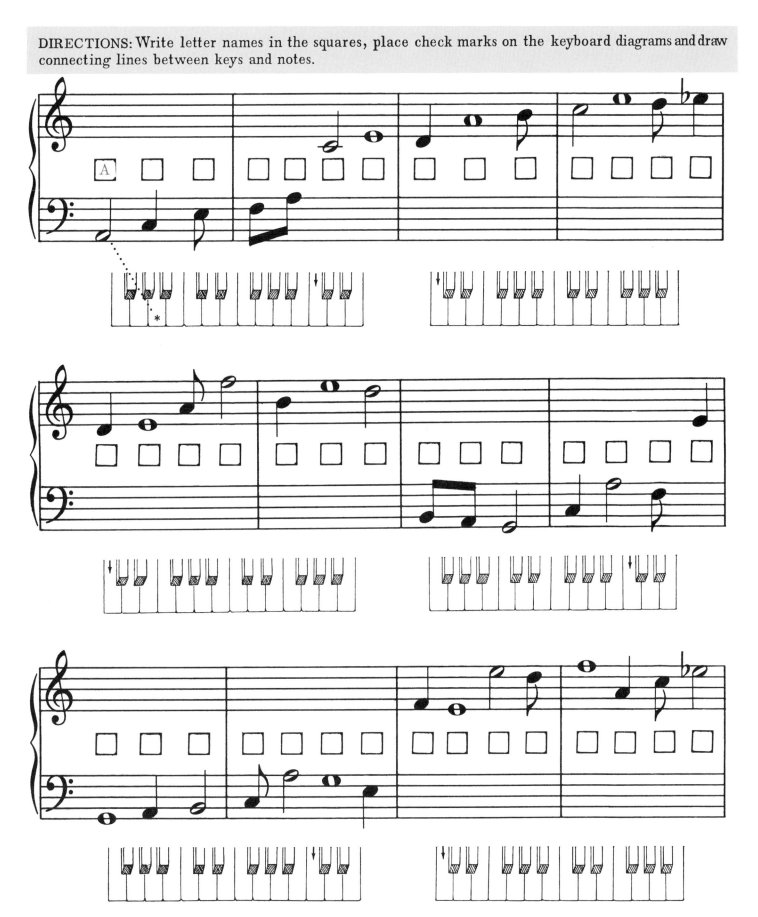

✔ Denotes Middle C

Lesson 6. Sharps, Flats, and Naturals

Pupil's Name..   *Completion Date*..

Assignment Date..   *Grade or Star*..

DIRECTIONS: On the staffs below you will find a series of sharps, flats and naturals. Place a whole note after each sign and write sharps, flats or naturals on the keyboard diagrams. Draw connecting lines between keys and notes.

↓ Denotes Middle C

Pupil's Name..   Completion Date..

Assignment Date..   Grade or Star..

DIRECTIONS: Study the LEGER lines and spaces in the first measure. Then, write letter names in the squares. Next, place check marks on the keyboard diagrams and draw connecting lines between keys and notes.

▼ Denotes Middle C

Lesson 8. Leger Lines and Spaces (Below Treble)

Pupil's Name.. Completion Date..

Assignment Date.. Grade or Star..

DIRECTIONS: Study the LEGER lines and spaces in the first measure. Then write letter names in the squares. Next, place check marks on the keyboard diagrams and draw connecting lines between keys and notes.

▼ Denotes Middle C

Pupil's Name .... *Completion Date* ....

Assignment Date .... *Grade or Star* ....

DIRECTIONS: Write letter names in squares, place check marks on keyboard diagrams, and draw connecting lines between keys and notes.

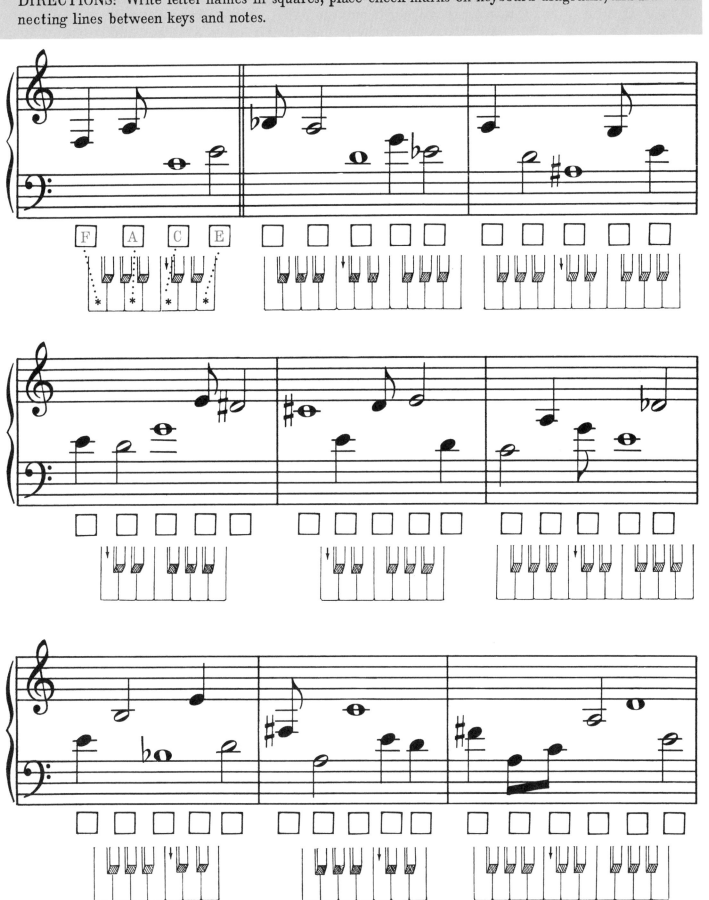

♦ Denotes Middle C

Lesson 10. Key Signature Spelling (Key of D)

Pupil's Name.. Completion Date..

Assignment Date.. Grade or Star...

DIRECTIONS: This lesson is in the key of D major which has two sharps: F♯ and C♯.   Remember to sharp every F and C unless cancelled by a natural sign (♮). Write letter names in the squares, place check marks on the keyboard diagrams and draw connecting lines between keys and notes.

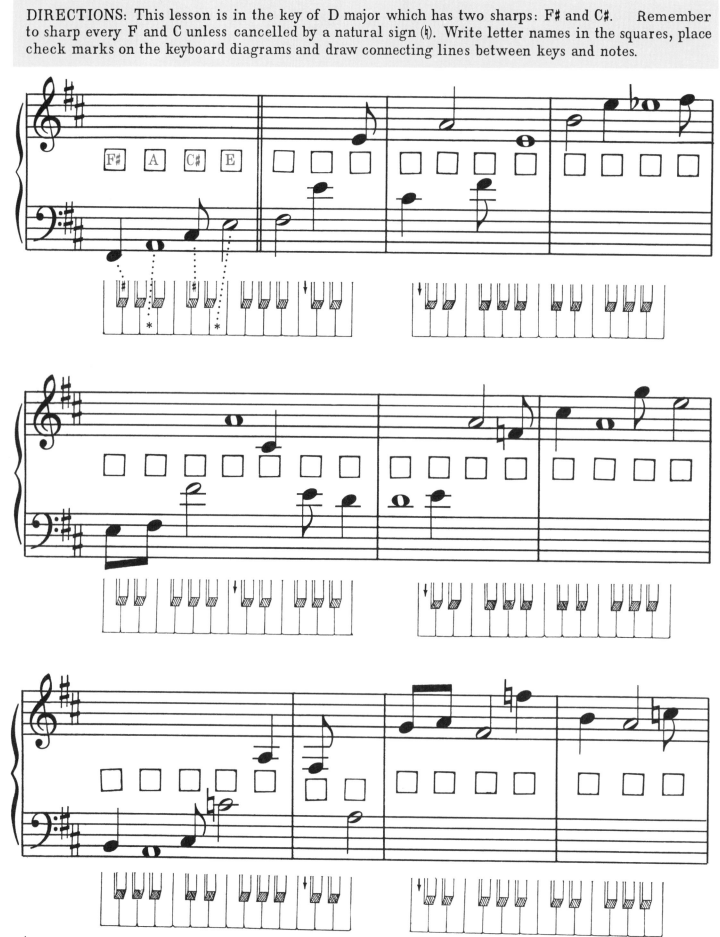

♦ Denotes Middle C

Pupil's Name..   Completion Date..

Assignment Date..   Grade or Star..

> DIRECTIONS: This lesson is in the key of B♭ major which has two flats: B♭ and E♭. Remember to flat every B and E unless cancelled by a natural sign (♮). Write letter names in the squares, place check marks on the keyboard diagrams and draw connecting lines between keys and notes.

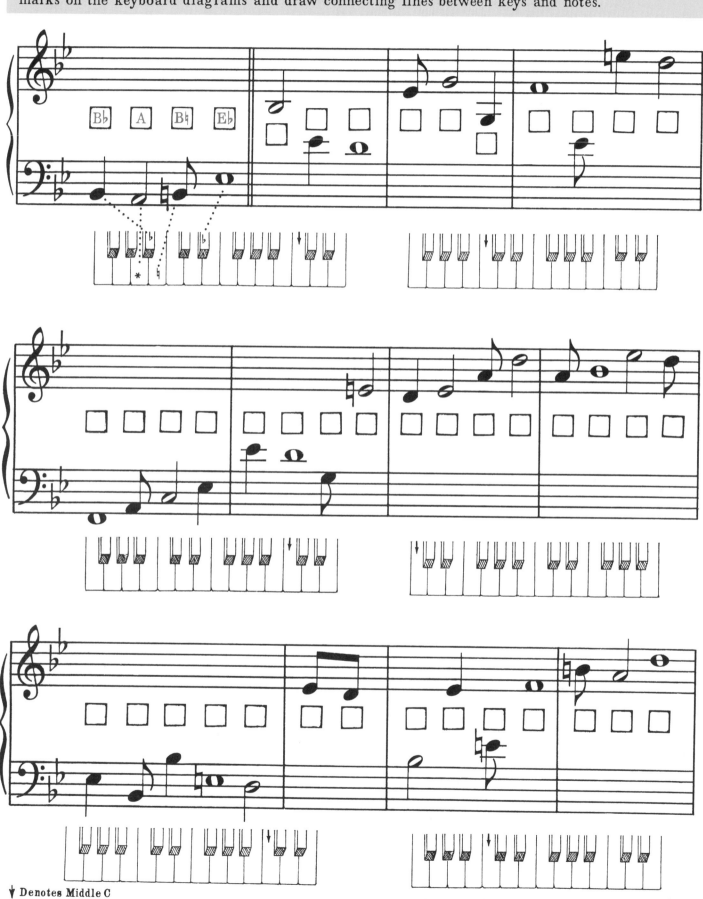

↓ Denotes Middle C

Lesson 12. Measure Tailoring (4/4 Time)

Pupil's Name.. Completion Date..

Assignment Date.. Grade or Star..

DIRECTIONS: Tailor the whole notes on the staffs below so that the total number of counts per measure is correct. A whole note can be tailored to any other type of note by one or more of the following ways: adding a stem, blackening the note head, attaching a flag to the stem, or adding a dot. For example, the THREE whole notes in the first measure can be tailored to ♩ ♩ ♩ or ♩. ♫; The TWO whole notes in the second measure can be altered to ♩ ♩ or ♩. ♩; After the counts are accurately totaled, write letter names in the squares.

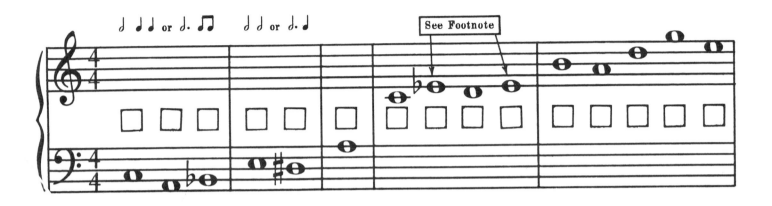

The RESTS in the following measures are to be included as part of the total number of counts. In the squares above or below the rests insert the fraction name as shown in measure No.1.

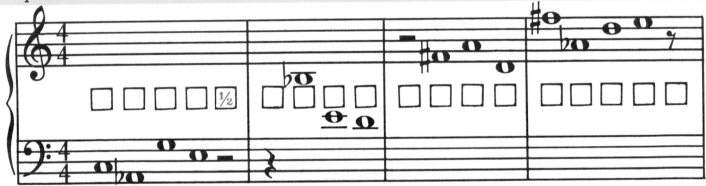

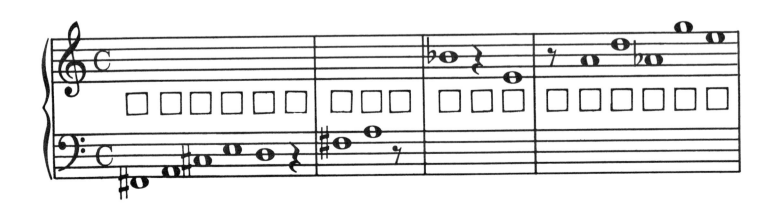

Note: A sharp, flat or natural (not in the key signature) applies to its particular note for the entire measure. A new measure cancels it.

Lesson 13. Measure Tailoring (3/4 Time)

Pupil's Name..   *Completion Date*..

Assignment Date..   *Grade or Star*..

DIRECTIONS: Tailor the whole notes on the staffs below so that the total number of counts in each measure is correct. After the counts are accurately totaled, write letter names in the squares.

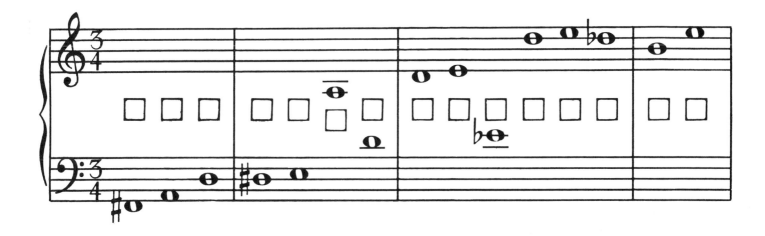

The RESTS in the following measures are to be included as part of the total number of counts. In the squares above or below the rests insert the fractional name as illustrated in the first measure.

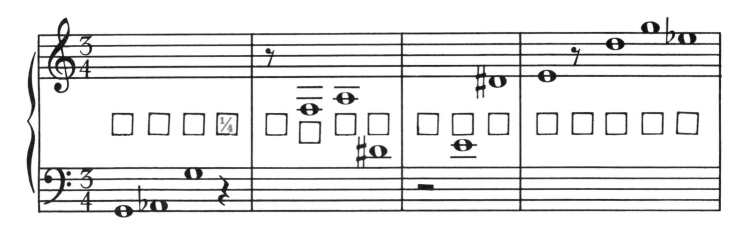

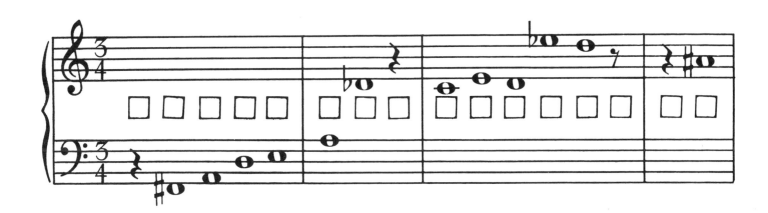

Lesson 14. Measure Tailoring (2/4 Time)

Pupil's Name.. Completion Date..

Assignment Date.. Grade or Star..

DIRECTIONS: Tailor the whole notes on the staffs below so that the total number of counts in each measure is correct. Include the rests whenever they appear. Occasionally a dotted quarter may be required. Consult the chart at the right. After the counts are accurately totaled, write letter names in the squares.

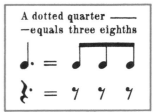

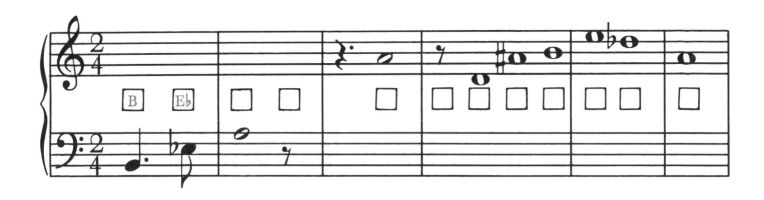

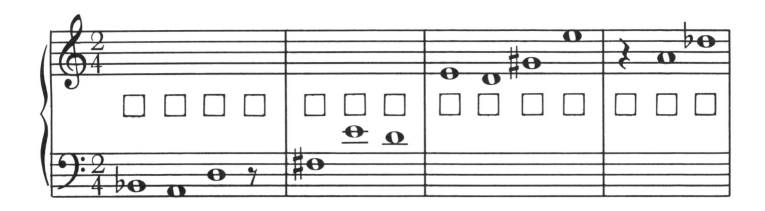

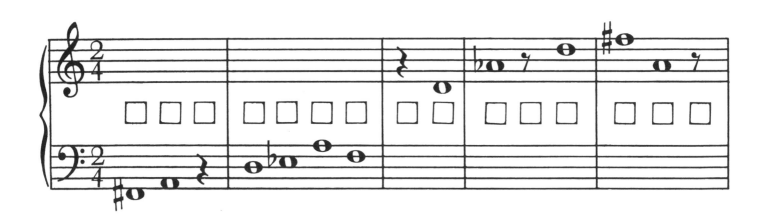

Pupil's Name...   *Completion Date*...

Assignment Date...   *Grade or Star*...

DIRECTIONS: Study the names of the leger lines and spaces in the first measure. Then write letter names in the squares. Next, place check marks on the keyboard diagrams and draw connecting lines between keys and notes.

Note: The small treble clef 𝄞 over C on the keyboard diagram denotes Treble C (first C above middle C).

Lesson 16. Leger Lines and Spaces (Below Bass)

DIRECTIONS: Study the names of the leger lines and spaces in the first measure. Then write letter names in the squares. Next, place check marks on the keyboard diagrams and draw connecting lines between keys and notes.

(See Footnote)

G A B C D E F G   C

Note: The small bass clef 𝄢 on the keyboard diagram denotes Bass C (first C below middle C)

Lesson 17. Widespread C-Hunt

Pupil's Name...   Completion Date...

Assignment Date...   Grade or Star...

Study the pattern of the six C's when the treble and bass staffs are placed vertically over the keyboard diagram. The two middle C's are one leger line INWARD from each staff. Then spreading OUTWARD in both directions the next two C's are located on the nearest space AWAY from each center staff line. Continuing OUTWARD, the next two C's are located on the SECOND leger line outside each staff.

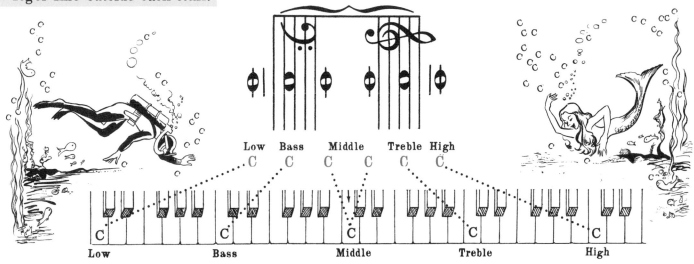

DIRECTIONS: Now for the C-Hunt. For each of the notes on the following staffs, place check marks on the keyboard diagrams and draw connecting lines between keys and notes.

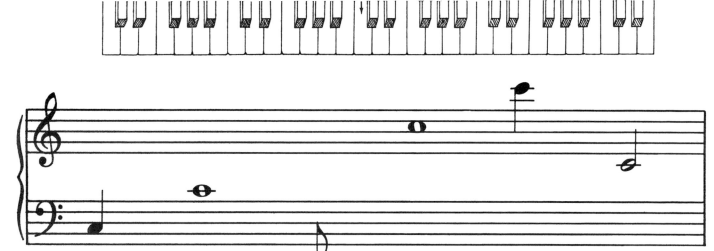

↓ Denotes Middle C

Lesson 18. Above and Below C-Level

Pupil's Name..

Completion Date..

Assignment Date..

Grade or Star..

The notes on the following four staffs represent four different C-levels. These four C's act as signals for music reading navigation.

DIRECTIONS: Write letter names in squares, place check marks on keyboard diagrams and draw connecting lines between keys and notes.

High C (Think: SECOND leger line above treble staff is SECOND C above middle C)

Treble C (Think: FIRST space above middle line is FIRST C above middle C)

Bass C (Think: FIRST space below middle line is FIRST C below middle C)

Low C (Think: SECOND leger line below bass staff is SECOND C below middle C)

The words "High C" over keyboard diagram indicate second C above middle C.

A small treble clef 𝄞 over C denotes Treble C (first C above middle C.)

A small bass clef 𝄢 over C indicates Bass C (first C below middle C.)

The words "Low C" over keyboard diagram denote second C below middle C.

Pupil's Name...   Completion Date...

Assignment Date...   Grade or Star...

DIRECTIONS: This lesson is in the key of A major which has three sharps: F#, C# and G#. Remember to sharp every F, C and G unless cancelled by a natural sign (♮). Write letter names in the squares, place check marks on the keyboard diagrams and draw connecting lines between keys and notes. (See Footnote)

C#   A   G#   E

Bass Clef

Note: The small treble clef 𝄞 over C on the keyboard diagram denotes Treble C (first C above middle C). The small bass clef 𝄢 over C indicates Bass C (first C below middle C).

Lesson 20. Harmonic Steps

Pupil's Name.. Completion Date..

Assignment Date.. Grade or Star..

There are two kinds of steps in music: melodic and harmonic. Melodic steps are sounded in succession, up or down. (See Examples 1 and 2.) Harmonic steps are sounded simultaneously as in Example 3. (See Teacher's note)

DIRECTIONS: In the squares under the harmonic steps, write the letter names, place check marks on the keyboard diagrams and draw connecting lines between keys and notes.

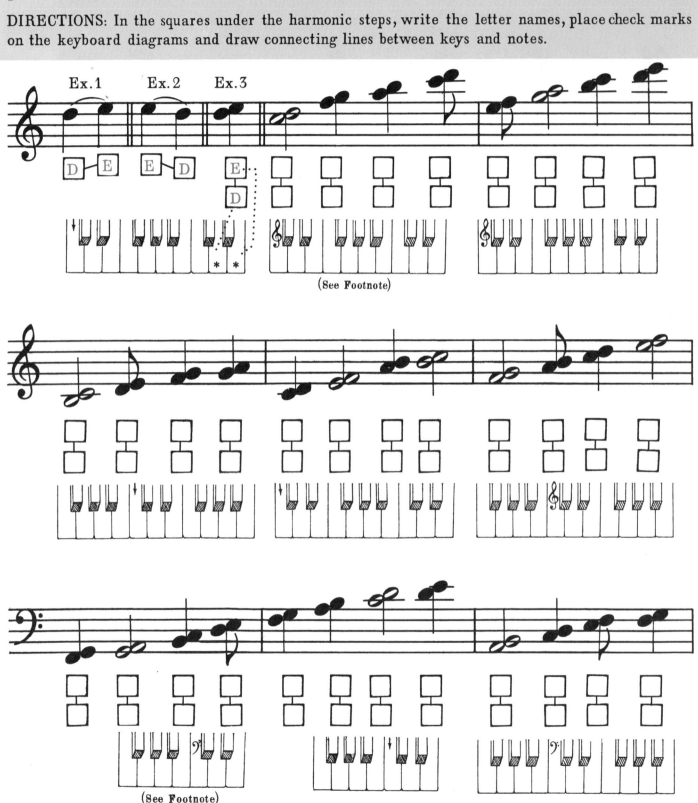

(See Footnote)

(See Footnote)

Teacher's Note: *Harmonic steps are presented from a reading and performance standpoint only. The theoretical significance of major and minor steps is purposely delayed.*

Note: The small treble clef 𝄞 over C on the keyboard diagram denotes Treble C (first C above middle C). The small bass clef 𝄢 over C indicates Bass C (first C below middle C).

↓ Denotes Middle C

Pupil's Name..   Completion Date..

Assignment Date...   Grade or Star...

There are two kinds of skips in music: melodic and harmonic. Melodic skips are sounded in succession, up or down. (See Examples 1 and 2.) Harmonic skips are sounded simultaneously as in Example 3.

DIRECTIONS: In the squares under the harmonic skips, write the letter names, place check marks on the keyboard diagrams and draw connecting lines between keys and notes.

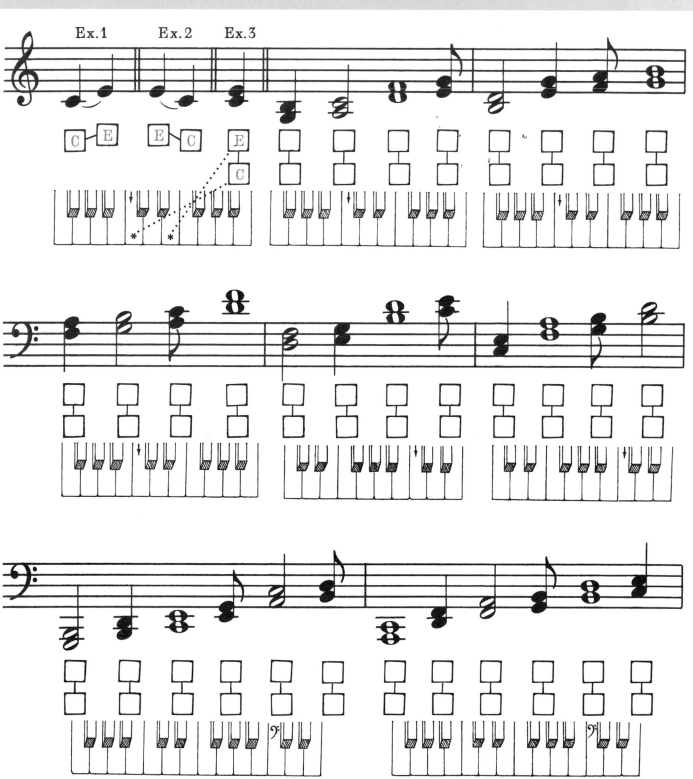

Ex.1   Ex.2   Ex.3

Note: The small bass clef 𝄢 over C on the keyboard diagram indicates **Bass C** (first C below middle C)

↓ Denotes Middle C

Lesson 22. Harmonic Intervals

Pupil's Name.. Completion Date..

Assignment Date.. Grade or Star..

An INTERVAL is the distance between two tones. Intervals are named according to their numerical size. In Example I (below) the interval is a FOURTH because it includes FOUR letter-names C-D-E-F. In Example II, the interval is a SIXTH because it includes SIX letter-names D-E-F-G-A-B. Each interval in this lesson is considered HARMONIC because both tones are sounded simultaneously.

DIRECTIONS: On the dotted lines above each of the following harmonic intervals, write the correct number names. To determine the number name, count the amount of letter-names proceeding from the lower tone to the upper tone. Count the lower note as "ONE" and continue counting until the upper tone is reached. Write letter-names in squares, place check marks on keyboard diagrams and draw connecting lines between keys and notes.

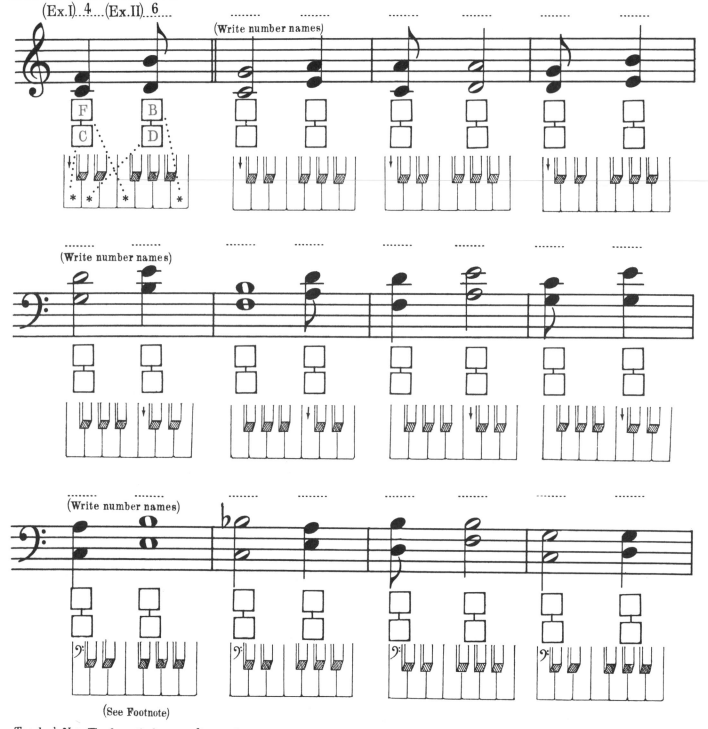

Teacher's Note: The theoretical aspect of intervals is intentionally delayed until the student acquires greater reading and performance ability.

Note: The small bass clef 𝄢 over C on the keyboard diagram indicates Bass-C (first C below middle C).

↓ Denotes Middle C

Pupil's Name.. Completion Date...

Assignment Date... Grade or Star...

DIRECTIONS: The following series of harmonic intervals include steps (seconds) and skips (thirds). Write number names on the dotted lines. Insert letter names in squares, place check marks on keyboard diagrams and draw connecting lines between keys and notes.

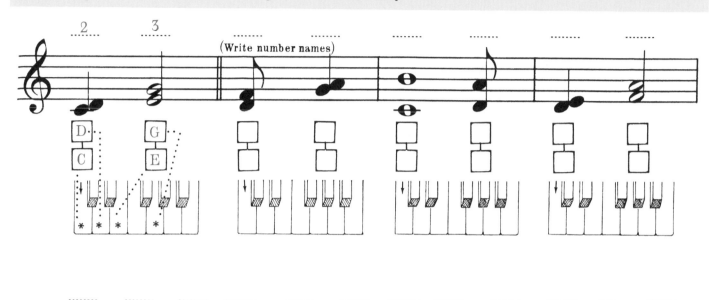

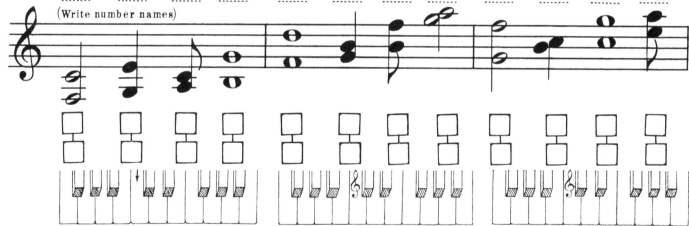

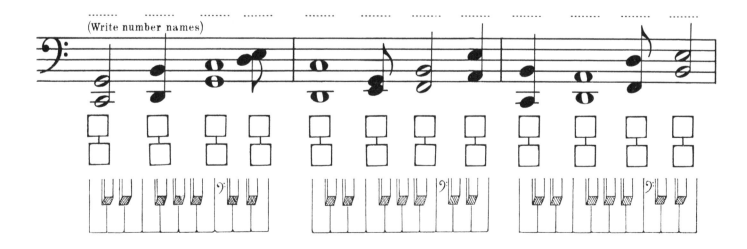

Note: The small treble clef 𝄞 over C on the keyboard diagram denotes Treble C (first C above middle C). The small bass clef 𝄢 over C indicates Bass C (first C below middle C). The arrow ↓ denotes middle C.

Lesson 24. Melodic Interval Recognition (Treble)

Pupil's Name..   Completion Date..

Assignment Date...   Grade or Star..

Melodic intervals are sounded in succession just like a MELODY is played. In fact, all melodies are made up of a series of melodic intervals.

DIRECTIONS: In each of the following melodies, join the notes with slurs. Insert letter names in squares and write the interval numbers on the dotted lines between the squares. Place check marks on the keyboard diagrams and draw connecting lines between keys and notes.

NOTE: The numerical size of an interval is never affected by the key signature, nor by any sharp, flat or natural which may be placed before it. Study the sample.

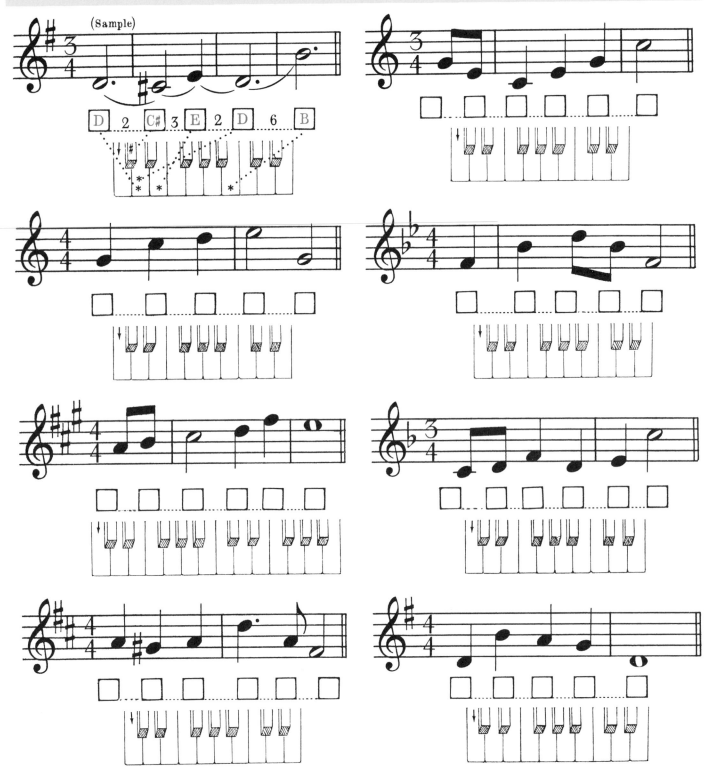

Teacher's Note: At this point, the student is to concentrate exclusively on the number names of the intervals. The theoretical varieties of intervals are intentionally delayed.

↓ Denotes Middle C

Pupil's Name...

Assignment Date...

Completion Date...

Grade or Star...

DIRECTIONS: In each of the following melodies, join the notes with slurs. Insert letter names in squares and write the interval numbers on the dotted lines between the squares. Place check marks on the keyboard diagrams and draw connecting lines between keys and notes.

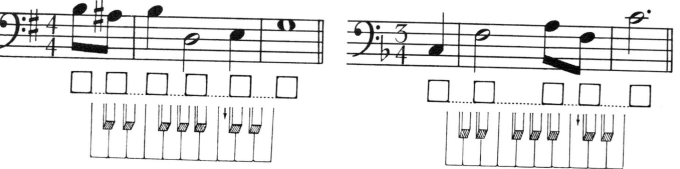

↓ Denotes Middle C

Lesson 26. Chords (Treble)

Pupil's Name .... Completion Date ....

Assignment Date .... Grade or Star ....

DIRECTIONS: A CHORD is a combination of three or more tones sounded simultaneously. In the following series of CHORDS, write letter names in squares, place check marks on keyboard diagrams and draw connecting lines between keys and notes. Study the sample.

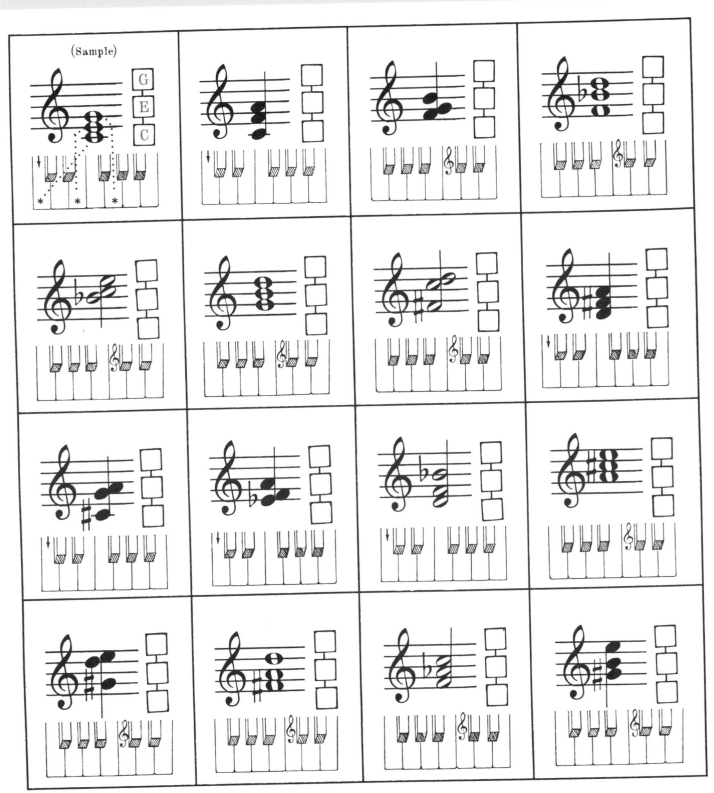

Teacher's Note: The theoretical and harmonic aspects of chords such as major and minor triads, inversions, seventh chords and other formations are intentionally delayed. Chord study at this point is to be devoted exclusively to STAFF READING and KEYBOARD LOCATION.

Note: The small treble clef 𝄞 over C on keyboard diagram indicates Treble C (first C above middle C).

↓ Denotes Middle C

Pupil's Name..   *Completion Date*..

Assignment Date..   *Grade or Star*..

DIRECTIONS: In the following series of CHORDS, write letter names in squares, place check marks on keyboard diagrams and draw connecting lines between keys and notes.

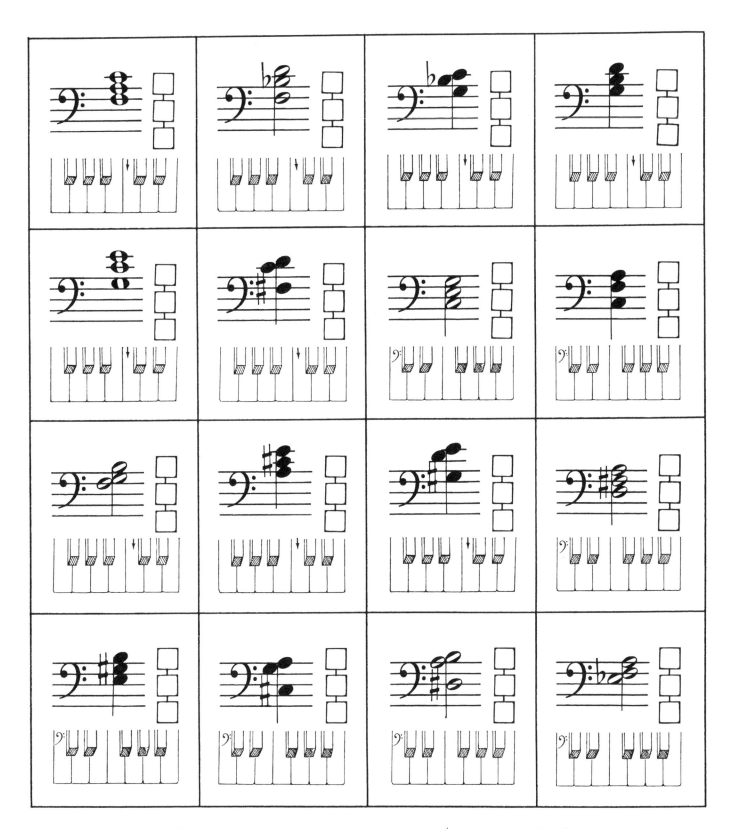

Note: The small bass clef 𝄢 over C on keyboard diagram indicates Bass C (first C below middle C).

↓ Denotes Middle C

Lesson 28. Musical Knowledge Quiz

Pupil's Name...   Completion Date...

Assignment Date..   Grade or Star...

DIRECTIONS: Below are twenty music questions. Five answers are given to each one. Study each question, then draw a line under the right answer. The sample is already correctly marked.

> Score 5 for each correct answer. A total score of 65 is passing, 70 is fair, 80 is good and 90 or above is excellent.

SAMPLE: This note 𝄞 is slogan word........ booster giant fast <u>gravity</u> globe

Score

1. This note 𝄞 is slogan word........... globe drives gravity encircles descent........ 1. ....

2. This note 𝄢 is slogan word........... brings fast booster earth's giant............... 2. ....

3. This note 𝄢 is slogan word........... gravity earth's drives flying encircles........ 3. ....

4. The word F-A-C-E represents................... { treble lines   bass spaces   treble spaces   bass lines   four four } .... 4. ....

5. This note 𝄢 is.................... D   F   B   F#   G .... 5. ....

6. This note 𝄞 is.................... Bb   G   D   C   F .... 6. ....

7. This note 𝄢 is.................... F   D   C#   F#   C .... 7. ....

8. This note 𝄞 is.................... B   D   G   Bb   Eb............ 8. ....

9. This measure 𝄞 ¾ needs.................... o   ♪   ♩   ♩   ♩.............. 9. ....

10. This measure 𝄢 ¾ needs.................... ♪   o   ♩.   ♩   ♩............. 10. ....

11. This measure 𝄞 ²⁄₄ needs.................... 𝄾   𝄽   𝄼   𝄻   𝄽.............. 11. ....

12. This measure 𝄢 ⁴⁄₄ needs.................... 𝄽   𝄾.   𝄻   𝄼   𝄾............. 12. ....

13. This note 𝄞 is .... Treble C Bass C Middle C High C Low C... 13. ....

14. This note 𝄢 is .... Low C High C Bass C Middle C Treble C... 14. ....

15. This 𝄞 is a................ { melodic interval   harmonic interval   chord   harmonic skip   melodic skip } .... 15. ....

16. This 𝄢 is a................................. 5th   3rd   6th   7th   4th .... 16. ....

17. This note 𝄞 is.................... F#   C#   G#   B   G .... 17. ....

18. This 𝄢 is a................................. 3rd   6th   5th   4th   2nd.......... 18. ....

19. The sharped note 𝄞 is...................... F#   G#   B#   A#   C#............ 19. ....

20. The flatted note 𝄢 is.................. Eb   Db   Gb   Bb   Ab......... 20 ....

Total Score   ....

You are now ready to progress to the Schaum SCALE SPELLER.

Music Spelling Bee

RULES: The Music Spelling Bee consists of three games as shown at the bottom. The games are designed for two students and are played with dice. The first step is to decide which game to play. The next step is to determine who is the first player and who is the second player. This is done by tossing a coin. Let's assume that Game No. 1 is selected. The first player rolls ONE of the dice. If, for example, the four side comes up ⚃ the first player spells the word GAGE on the large staffs. This is done by placing small buttons, beans, or candies on the lines or spaces that correctly spell the word. Then the second player rolls one of the dice. If the four side comes up ⚃ the second

player spells the word FACE. Thus, the game rotates between the two players, each spelling the word called by the number on the die. The first player who spells all the words in his column is the winner. In case a player rolls one of the dice and a number comes up calling for a word that he has previously spelled, that player loses his turn. If a player spells a word incorrectly, he forfeits the word and loses a turn. The game may be varied by spelling the words entirely in the treble or entirely in the bass, or alternately. Another variation could consist of doing all the spelling on the leger lines or leger spaces, or alternately. Many other adaptations are possible.

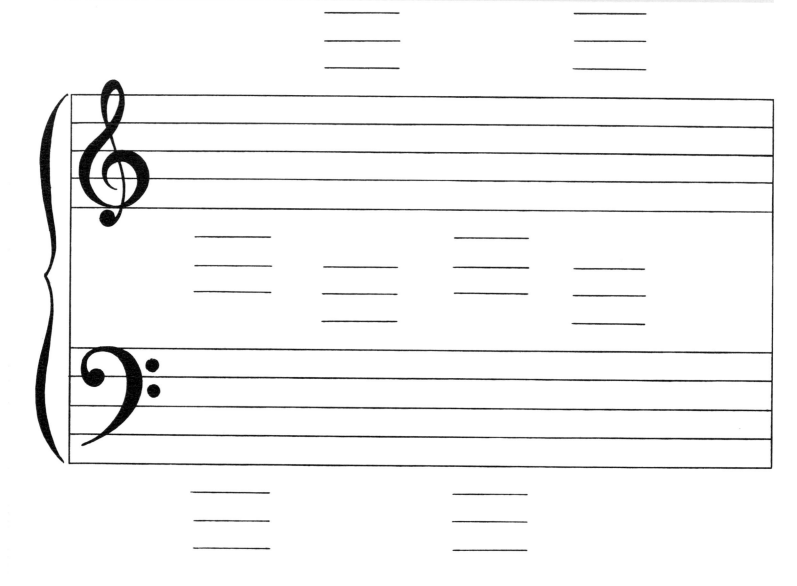

Game No. 1
FOUR-LETTER WORDS

1st Player	2nd Player
⚀ BADE	⚀ AGED
⚁ DEED	⚁ CEDE
⚂ ABED	⚂ BAFF
⚃ GAGE	⚃ FACE
⚄ BEAD	⚄ CAGE
⚅ EDGE	⚅ CAFE

Game No. 2
FIVE-LETTER WORDS

1st Player	2nd Player
⚀ FACED	⚀ ADAGE
⚁ ABACA	⚁ EBBED
⚂ EDGED	⚂ BADGE
⚃ GADGE	⚃ ADDED
⚄ FADED	⚄ CEDED
⚅ EGGED	⚅ CAGED

Game No. 3
SIX-LETTER WORDS

1st Player	2nd Player
⚀ ACCEDE	⚀ BEEFED
⚁ BEGGED	⚁ DECADE
⚂ EFFACE	⚂ FACADE
⚃ BAGGED	⚃ DEFACE
⚄ DEEDED	⚄ BEADED
⚅ FACADE	⚅ GAGGED

Successful Schaum Sheet Music

This is a Partial List –– Showing Level 1 through Level 2

✋ = 5 Finger Position   * = Big Notes   • = Original Form   ✓ = Chord Symbols

ACTION SOLOS

			LEVEL
52-07 *•	ASTRONAUT ADVENTURE (L. H. Melody)	Schaum	1
52-25 *•	BUBBLE BLUES	Weston	1
55-20 *	POGO STICK CHOP (Based on "Chop Sticks")	Schaum	2
55-34 •	RIGHT ON (Staccato)	Miller	2
55-26 •	WATER SLIDE (Staccato)	Payne	2

AMERICAN – PATRIOTIC SOLOS

55-14	AMERICA THE BEAUTIFUL	Ward	2
55-41	MARINES' HYMN	Traditional	2
55-08	WABASH CANNON BALL	Railroad Song	2

ANIMALS and BIRDS

52-16 *•	BUSY WOODPECKER ✋ (Staccato)	Cahn	1
52-36 •	DINOSAUR LAND	Schaum	1
55-54 •	EQUESTRIAN PROCESSION	Cahn	2
52-38 •	KANGAROO HOP ✋	Polk	1
52-24 *•	PERKY TURKEY	Weston	1
55-09 *•	POPPO the PORPOISE (L. H. Melody)	Littlewood	2

BOOGIE

55-07 *•	COOL SCHOOL (Boogie Style)	Schaum	2
55-02 •	LITTLE DOG BOOGIE	Schaum	2

BOTH HANDS in TREBLE CLEF

52-27 •	JOYOUS BELLS ✋ (with Duet Accomp.)	Cahn	1
55-56 •	MUSIC BOX LULLABY	Levin	2
55-44 •	MYSTICAL ETUDE (Staccato)	Cahn	2

CHRISTMAS

70-10 *	IT CAME UPON THE MIDNIGHT CLEAR	Trad.	1
81-06	LITTLE DRUMMER BOY, The	Arr. Schaum	1
81-07	SANTA CLAUS IS COMIN' TO TOWN	Arr. Schaum	1
70-02	TWELVE DAYS of CHRISTMAS	All 12 Verses	1
70-01 *	WHAT CHILD IS THIS? ("Greensleeves")	Trad.	1

CIRCUS

55-39 •	CIRCUS PONIES	Leach	2
55-58 •	CLOWN WALTZ	Kitchen	2
55-53 •	RINGMASTER'S MARCH	Cahn	2

CLASSICS

52-09 *	Beethoven . SONG of JOY ("Ode To Joy" from 9th Symph.)		1
52-37	Grieg ...... In the HALL of the MOUNTAIN KING		1
52-12 ✓	Handel .... HALLELUJAH CHORUS (Easy Edition)		1
55-30	Mozart MOZART'S ROMANCE ("A Little Night Music")		2
55-45	Pachelbel ....PACHELBEL'S CANON (Easy Edition)		2
52-35	Rossini .... WILLIAM TELL MARCH		1

COUNTRY/WESTERN

55-35	DAGGER DANCE ("Land of Sky Blue Waters")	Herbert	2
52-06 *•	PONY RIDE ✋	McCreary	1

DESCRIPTIVE MUSIC

52-39 •	ANCIENT PAGODA	Biel	1
52-43 *•	BE A STAR ✋	Rita	1
55-46	COME BACK TO SORRENTO	deCurtis	2
55-47 •	DOMINOES	Cahn	2
52-32 *•	GLIDING ON THE WIND	Hampton	1
52-44 *•	GOING BY, MERRILY	Rita	1
55-49 •	IN A FAR OFF TIME & PLACE	Revezoulis	2
52-42 *•	IT'S FUN TO LEARN ✋	Rita	1
52-40 •	JOLLY LEPRECHAUN	Revezoulis	1
52-46 •	JUST IMAGINE IT	Rita	1
55-51 •	PEACEFUL INTERLUDE	Holmes	2
55-42 •	SUNSET SERENADE	Levin	2

DUET (1 Piano, 4 Hands)

			LEVEL
71-02	PARADE of the TOY SOLDIERS	Jessel	1
71-07	HARK the HERALD ANGELS SING	Traditional	2

FOOD

55-38 •	HURRY, LITTLE PIZZA CAR	Holmes	2

HALLOWEEN

55-40 *•	GALLOPING GHOSTS (Minor Key)	Weston/Schaum	2
55-57 *•	TRICK OR TREAT PARADE	Rita	2
52-15 *•	SPOOK HOUSE (L. H. Melody)	Schaum	1
52-20 *•	SPUNKY SPOOKS (Both Hands in Bass)	Weston	1

JAZZ STYLE

55-48 •	DUDE	Weston	2

LEFT HAND MELODY

52-22 •	KNOCKING AT MY DOOR ✋	Schaum	1
55-50 •	SCOTTISH SKETCH	Holmes	2

MARCHES

52-34 •	FANFARE	King	1
55-06	PARADE of the TOY SOLDIERS	Jessel	2

MINOR KEY

55-52•	DREAM CATCHER	Holmes	2
52-28 •	SECRET AGENT	Weston	1

MOVIE THEME

80-01	STAR WARS (Main Title)	Williams	2

OLDIES but GOODIES

52-21 ✓	SCHOOL DAYS	Edwards	1

RAGTIME

55-21 *✓	ENTERTAINER (Easy Version)	Joplin	2
55-55 •	RICKETY RAG	Schaum	2

SACRED

55-25 *✓	HOW GREAT THOU ART	Swedish Folk Melody	2

SPORTS/LEISURE

52-10 *•	CHEERLEADER	Plank	1
52-45 *•	DAD'S DUNE BUGGY	Turner	1
52-18 *•	JOGGING TRAIL ✋ (Minor Key)	Payne	1
55-43 •	ROLLER BLADES	Schaum	2
52-41 •	SKI TRAILS	King	1
55-28 ✓	TAKE ME OUT TO THE BALL GAME	Von Tilzer	2

SPRINGTIME

55-18 *•	FAWN'S LULLABY	Masson	2
52-04 *	SPRING, SWEET SPRING	Lincke	1
52-31 *•	TREES IN THE BREEZE	Hampton	1

STACCATO

55-23 *•	FRISKY FROG (Both Hands in Treble)	Cahn	2
52-33 •	HOPSCOTCH	Hampton	1
52-11 *•	WINDSHIELD WIPER ROCK (Staccato)	Noblitt	1

THANKSGIVING

52-24 *•	PERKY TURKEY	Weston	1
55-12	THANKSGIVING SCENE	Medley of 4 Hymns	2

WALTZES

52-30 •	OPUS ONE	Cahn	1